You *Can* Drive a Porsche

Life's too short not to

Philip Raby

You *Can* Drive a Porsche

First published 2011. This edition published 2017

Copyright © Philip Raby 2017

All rights reserved.

Published by Solid Air Publishing

All rights reserved. No part of this publication may be reproduced in any form without the prior written permission of the author.

All recommendations within this book are made without any guarantee on the part of the author or publisher, who also disclaim any liability incurred in connection with the use of this book.

www.philipraby.co.uk

Introduction

Thanks for buying this little book. There have been countless other books written about Porsches, but most are aimed at enthusiasts and go into great detail about the history of the cars, the minute differences between various models, and the mechanical specifications.

This book is a bit different, though. It's aimed at the newcomer to the marque – someone who's always wanted a Porsche but knows nothing about them. It gives a gentle introduction to Porsche and guides you through the minefield of the various affordable models.

Many people think that you have to be rich to drive a Porsche, yet they unwittingly waste money buying and driving a mundane car when, in fact, they could own the Porsche of their dreams for less long-term outlay.

This book will change the way you think about car ownership and includes the following information:

• The difference between foolish and clever car buyers.

• A Porsche can be less expensive to own than a modern saloon car.

You *Can* Drive a Porsche

• Porsches are environmentally friendly.

• A gentle introduction to the many models of Porsche

• Which Porsches make a good first buy.

If you thought that Porsche ownership was only a dream, then it's time to think again.

I hope this book encourages you to think differently about how you buy and run your cars, and unleashes you to realise your dream. It may even make you think differently about how you organise your finances in general.

You'll discover that owning a Porsche is a lot of fun and something anyone can afford to do.

Philip Raby

Chapter one
Realising the dream

Children are great, aren't they? They've not had time to become brainwashed into limiting their potential. Ask a child what they want to do for a living when they grow up and, so long as they're not in a 'dunno' mood, they'll regale you with plans of being a rock star, racing driver, actor, astronaut, airline pilot, or something else just as exciting. They'll tell you about the fantastic house they'll live in, with 20 bedrooms, ensuite Jacuzzis and high-definition televisions in each of the many toilets. And, of course, they'll drive a very cool car.

Be honest, now, you probably had similar dreams when you were a child. Sadly, though, over the years those dreams were bashed out of you by parents, teachers, friends and, well, the realities of life. Maybe that's inevitable; after all, there are rather more openings in life for accountants than there are for astronauts.

There are countless books available that promise to tell you how to realise your full potential

You *Can* Drive a Porsche

and become the multimillionaire you always wanted to be; so long as you retrain your inner self, take up meditation, talk to your hamster in a certain way, or sell lots of washing powder. This book, however, has a rather more modest – and a much more achievable – aim. It will show you how you can afford to drive the car of your dreams. And the good news is, you don't need to earn any more money than you do today. In fact, you may end up saving money.

What was your dream car when you were a child? A Ferrari? A Lamborghini? A Porsche? I'm betting it was a Porsche, for the simple reason you're reading this book. And I also bet that it was a Porsche 911 because that's the model everyone aspires to own. In fact, you may well have had a poster of a 911 Turbo on your bedroom wall.

Now, look outside and see what's parked on your drive? I suspect it's not a Porsche – if it were, you wouldn't need this book. I reckon it's something mundane, like a Ford Mondeo or Vauxhall Astra. Oh dear, hardly the stuff of your childhood dreams, is it?

Why isn't there a Porsche sitting out there, then? You're going to say it's because you can't afford to buy and run a Porsche, aren't you? Well, I'm going to tell you that there's a good chance that the mundane saloon car parked on your drive is costing you more than a Porsche would.

You *Can* Drive a Porsche

Of course, you may well drive a more impressive car, perhaps a smart BMW or a brand new sports car. Very nice, but you could still be driving a Porsche that would cost you less money in the long term.

Foolish Car Buyers

Let's meet Mark. Mark is a schoolteacher and a thoroughly sensible chap with his money. He knows exactly how much he earns and how much he has to spend each month. He puts a modest amount into his pension and sets some money aside for a rainy day (or, more likely, for the day the boiler blows up). He never goes overdrawn and he pays off his credit card bill in full each month. Like I said, he's sensible with his money. So why does he get it all so wrong with his cars?

Mark always buys a brand-new hatchback every three years. "I like the reassurance of a manufacturer's warranty because, once a car's out of warranty, things start to go wrong," he explains. Umm, that's a shaky argument – today's cars are, on the whole, thoroughly reliable. I know someone who drives a 15-year-old Nissan and, despite having covered over 100,000 miles and rarely getting any love or attention, the old rice-burner has never, ever let him down. In fact, a brand-new car is more likely to suffer from teething problems.

You *Can* Drive a Porsche

You may think that Mark is, as is his nature, being cautious and sensible, but let's just look at the facts.

His latest hatchback had a showroom price of around £15,000. It's nothing fancy, but it is all shiny and new, has that lovely new-car smell inside, was sold to him by a nice man in a suit and, of course, comes with that all important warranty that Mark is so keen on. Sounds perfect until you realise that, in fact, the car is going to cost him not £15,000 but actually – wait for it – £25,500, plus servicing and maintenance. Gosh, what's happened to Mark's sensible approach to life?

Well, Mark is a classic example of a Foolish Car Buyer. To find out why he is, we have to do some maths but don't worry; it's nothing too arduous.

First of all, Mark is on a modest teacher's salary; he's by no means poor but he just doesn't have £15,000 hidden under the pillow to pay for his new car. So he takes out a loan from the bank – being the steady fellow he is, he'd rather deal with his bank than get involved in finance deals. Now, at the time of writing, a typical car loan from a UK bank would attract an interest rate of about 6.5 percent APR, which means that, over three years, Mark would pay about £1500 in interest. To be fair, that isn't a bad deal in itself, but it does take the cost of the car to £16,500 (I'm rounding these figures off, by the way, to keep things neat).

You *Can* Drive a Porsche

Now, although that's not great news, it's realistic to assume that not many of us are in the happy position to fork out £15,000 or so in hard cash, so we can't really criticise Mark for borrowing the money, can we?

Where things began to go wrong for our hapless teacher, though, is when he proudly drove his shiny new hatchback out of the showroom. As the suited salesman started thinking about how to spend his bonus, Mark immediately began to lose money. Big time. Why? Because his new car had suddenly become a second-hand car, and second-hand (or 'pre-owned' in dealer-speak) cars are worth less than new ones. If Mark had tried to sell his car the very next day he probably would have lost a couple of thousand on it.

And the drop in value – or depreciation to use the technical term for this evil – continues. A typical car like Mark's will lose about 40 percent of its value in its first year of life alone, which means it would be worth about £9000 within 12 months. Ouch! By the end of the second year, the car would have dropped in value by over 50 percent and, by the time Mark's precious three-year warranty has expired, his car would have lost 60 percent of its new value. In other words, it would now be worth just £6000. Great news for the person who buys it from him, but bad news for Mark. If you learn nothing else from this book, just remember that you're better off purchasing a three-year-old car than a brand-new one!

Factor in the interest on the loan and Mark's mundane hatchback has actually cost him a total of £25,500, plus the usual servicing and maintenance; say, £1200 over three years. Wow, now you can see why he's a Foolish Car Buyer. Mark will, of course, point out that the car still has some value – around £6000 – so it's not actually cost him that much. Fair point, until you realise that he's about to trade the car in for an even lower value than that (he can't be bothered to sell it himself so will have to accept a trade-in figure from the local main dealer) and repeat the whole fruitless exercise. Oh, and for the record, Mark is an economics teacher...

Don't think that this madness is limited to teachers, though; most car buyers follow the same cycle. Take the case of James, a successful solicitor who likes to spend money and enjoy life to the full while, at the same time, investing carefully in shares and property to build a secure future for himself. James drives a rather nice BMW 3 Series and he feels pleased with himself because it's one of the UK's slowest depreciating cars, losing just 25 percent of its value in the first year. Indeed, being a bright fellow, this was one of the reasons he chose the car.

You *Can* Drive a Porsche

The trouble is, the car's showroom price was £27,000 and he then added a hefty £5000 of options – it's all too easy to get away ticking boxes when you're ordering a new car – and these made very little difference to the second-hand (sorry, pre-owned) value. So, after a year, the BMW had dropped in value by a quarter of £27,000 plus the £5000 option bill. In other words, the car James had spent £32,000 on when new was now worth less than £19,000.

After three years, the BMW was worth just £13,000, so James had now lost an eye-watering £20,000 in that short time – and that's just in depreciation.

The story only gets worse, mind. Like Mark, James didn't have the money to pay cash for his new car – in fact, very few car buyers do – and personal loans only go up to £25,000, so he chose to put down £8000 cash from the same of his old car and borrow the balance. The interest on that amount over three years added £2600 to the cost of James' car so, in the end, the BMW cost a staggering £55,600. Being a solicitor, he should know when he's being ripped off. Sadly, though, he just proved himself to be yet another Foolish Car Buyer – this time with bells on. As with Mark, James could have sold the car at the end of the period and recouped £13,000 but he'd still be £42,000 down on the deal and, having an image to maintain, he would have to go out and buy another, probably even more expensive, car, thus repeating the cycle.

It seems crazy that most people are prepared to go through life throwing money away like this. After all, they wouldn't dream of buying a house in this way. Quite the opposite, in fact – sensible home buyers always consider carefully whether or not their purchase will be a good, long-term investment. The difference is, people expect their homes to go up in value, or appreciate, while they accept that their cars will drop in value – the dreaded depreciation. However, few actually realise – or are too scared to face up to – just how much money they lose on their cars. Foolish Car Buyers, the lot of them!

Clever Car Buyers

Let's go back to houses. If you're smart, you'll think carefully when you buy a home, choosing somewhere in a good district and perhaps with potential for improvement, so that you can be confident that, when the time comes, you'll be able to sell it quickly. You certainly won't expect to lose money on the deal but, ideally, you'll hope to make a few bob.

However, even if you don't worry too much about making money on your home, the chances are you will. That's because houses are considered to be assets – a long-lasting product that, so long as it's well maintained, should outlast you. A house, then, is deemed to be an investment, which is one reason when banks charge less for mortgages than for other loans – they know they can get the money back by repossessing the property if you are unable to pay.

Wouldn't it be great if cars could be like this? Well, while most cars are never going to be a rock-solid investment in the same way as property has in the UK since the Second World War (despite dips, values have steadily risen over the long-term), Clever Car Buyers do consider their car purchases in a similar way to their property deals.

Take Carl as an example. Carl lives in a neat five-bedroomed house; it's nothing too fancy but it's larger than most of his friends' homes and – here's the key – he's only got a relatively small mortgage compared to the value of the property. How has he managed this? By buying smart and moving up the property ladder, starting with a tiny two-bedroomed cottage. He's always bought houses in respectable areas and has been prepared to roll up his sleeves and get his hands dirty improving his homes. Over 15 years he has moved six times, gradually working his way up to his present home and, not surprisingly, he's planning his next move soon.

You *Can* Drive a Porsche

Carl works as a manager in a local retail store and is an enigma to his friends and neighbours. They know he doesn't earn a large salary yet, not only does he live in a decent home, but he also drives a Porsche 911. Not because he's flash – far from it – but because he loves the shape of the cars and the way they drive. Like many of us, he dreamt of owning a 911 since he was a child and finally realised his dream.

However, there is another reason that Carl drives a 911. And that's because he views his car like his home – as a durable item that he gets repaired on the odd occasion it goes wrong, and something that won't cost him a lot of money.

Let's look at the figures. Carl bought his 2001 Porsche three years ago for £15,000 – the same price as Mark's hatchback. Unlike Mark, though, he didn't have to borrow the money because he'd previously been driving an older car with little value (a beat-up Volvo estate that was ideal for lugging building materials around) and his mortgage is small, so he was able to save up each month.

That was three years ago, and do you know what Carl's Porsche is worth today? About £15,000! That's because the car has done most of its depreciating and values are relatively stable. People want to buy 911s, so there's a healthy market for them, especially good, well-maintained examples like Carl's.

You *Can* Drive a Porsche

Ah, I hear you say, but surely that maintenance will be higher than for Mark's new hatchback. Yes, of course it will be – a typical service is about twice the price and Carl's had to spend money on things like a new clutch and brakes. He treats his Porsche like his home; fixing any problems to ensure it keeps running indefinitely. Over the three years, the car has cost him around £4000 in maintenance, compared to Mark's car which cost £1200 to service over the same period.

But, compare that to the massive loss of almost £20,000 Mark made during the time he owned his hatchback, and the cost of running a Porsche suddenly becomes rather modest. Indeed, you'd be very unlucky, indeed, to have to spend anything like £20,000 on maintaining any car.

Let's meet another Clever Car Buyer – a marketing specialist by the name of Tim. Tim really is clever in that he drives a lovely 1995 911 worth about £45,000 – and he doesn't owe a penny on it. Now, Tim is reasonably well paid but he's by no means wealthy enough to have that sort of money sitting around in the bank, so how did he manage to buy such a great car?

The answer is he's done just what Carl did with houses, only with Porsches. Tim started with a 1982 911SC that he bought for £15,000, using money he'd saved up. He then sold that car for £17,000 just six months later and bought a slightly

You *Can* Drive a Porsche

younger 911 for £19,000 and, again, sold that on promptly for £22,000. He kept on doing this, adding the odd £1000 now and then, to work his way up the ladder. A year ago he sold a 1991 911 Carrera 4 for £40,000 (a car he'd bought for £30,000) and then paid £40,000 for his present Porsche, and he's already been offered £45,000 for that one.

Now that really is Clever Car Buying! How does he do it? By buying cars cheaply – he's good at sniffing out bargains and negotiating a good deal. At first, he bought cars that needed a bit of tidying, but now only buys good examples at the right price. When it comes to selling, Tim uses his marketing skills to promote the car in the best light – with clear photographs and descriptive text – and in the best places.

The only problem Tim has now is that he's realised his dream – the 993 is the car he's always wanted and he's no real desire to own a newer 911! He's also bought smart, in that his car is one of the most desirable 911s ever and so should hold its value very well, indeed.

Like I said, he's a Clever Car Buyer and in the following chapters I'll show how you can be, too.

You *Can* Drive a Porsche

Which Porsche to buy?

Let's be honest here, the Porsche everyone really wants is a 911, isn't it? I talk to people all the time who drive 944s and Boxsters, and they inevitably tell me that they want a 911 one day.

Now, don't get me wrong, I've nothing against 944s, Boxsters, Caymans and the like – I've had a lot of fun driving all sorts of Porsches – but there is something about the 911 which makes it the stuff of dreams. Maybe it's the shape, the sound, the 50-plus years of history, its motorsport heritage – or, most likely, a mixture of all that.

To realistically buy a 911, you need at least £13,000, which will get you behind the wheel of a decent example from the late 1990s to early 2000s. Sure, you can buy 911s for less than that but, unless you know what you're letting yourself in for, you could get your fingers burnt. If a car is too cheap, there has to be a reason – and that reason is usually that there is something wrong with it. Which means that it needs money – perhaps lots – spending on it.

You *Can* Drive a Porsche

Buy the right 911 and it will hold its value well, but buy badly and you could end up being out of pocket. Of course, spending more doesn't guarantee that you'll get a good example but, generally speaking, you should steer clear of ultra-cheap Porsches, whatever the age and model.

So if a 911 is beyond you, look around at other Porsches, such as a Boxster or, going back further in time, a 944 or 924. These are superb cars and you can have a lot of fun with one. Again, though, do steer clear of those at the bottom end of the market, unless you find a real bargain that you can just run around in until it dies.

The following chapters give more information on the various models of Porsche that you can consider buying.

Nine *what?*

Porsche model names and numbers can be very confusing to the newcomer to the marque. When is a Porsche 911 not a 911? When it's a Carrera, a GT2 or a GT3. Or maybe when it's a 964, 993, 996 or 997. It can be highly confusing.

Let's get one thing clear, then – basically anything that has a 911 shape and a flat-six engine in the back is a 911. Flat-six, incidentally, refers to the engine's configuration – six cylinders laid flat, three on each side.

So where do all the 964s, 993s and 996s come in? Well, these are actually Porsche's internal model numbers – the cars were never sold as such, but the numbers have become a useful way of identifying the many different types of 911s. Here's a quick rundown of 911 model numbers you're likely to come across:

964: The 911 models sold from 1989 to 1993.

965: Sometimes incorrectly used to identify the 964-model 911 Turbo, but actually a long-forgotten Porsche prototype.

993: The 911 models sold from 1994 to 1998.

996: The all-new, water-cooled 911 range sold from 1998 to 2005.

997: The revised 911 range sold from 2005.

991: The all-new 911 introduced in 2012.

Oddly, for many years most 911s (with the exception of some special editions) haven't been badged as such since the 911SC went out of production in 1993. Instead, they've carried a 'Carrera' script on the rear. They are still 911s, though. It's good to see that Porsche has finally reintroduced the '911' badge on the 991.

By the way, while we're on the subject, you may also see Boxsters referred to as 986 (1997 to 2004), 987 (2004 to 2012) and 981 (2012-2016); again, these are Porsche's internal designations. Just to throw a spanner in the works, however, from 2016, the Boxster and Cayman have both been badged as '718'.

You may also see people on the Internet referring to '996TT' and '997TT'. This is an odd way of naming the 996 and 997 Turbos – the cars have twin turbochargers, hence the 'TT'. It's not an official designation, though, and one I think should remain with Audis.

911SC and 3.2 Carrera

The earliest 911 I'd recommend to a first-time Porsche buyer is an SC (although I may be biased because my first 911 was an SC!). These were built from 1978 to 1983 and featured a 3.0-litre engine that produced 180bhp on the first cars, rising to 204bhp in 1981.

I like the SC because it has the looks and character of older 911s with less of the hassles. The bodyshell was fully galvanised so rust is less of a problem (note the word 'less' here – I'll come back to this) and the engine is well-sorted, making it tough and reliable. It's also a gloriously free-revving and torquey powerplant, making an SC a lot of fun to drive.

It's also a relatively simple car from a mechanical point of view, so a good one shouldn't be expensive to maintain, while most parts are readily available.

For many years, the SC was a little bit unloved and, as a result, was a very affordable 911, which prices as low as £10,000. Not anymore, though.

You *Can* Drive a Porsche

People have begun to appreciate what great cars 911SCs are, and there aren't that many good ones left. That means prices have skyrocketed, and you'll be lucky to find one for less than £30,000, with good examples selling for in excess of £40,000. Some smart car buyers have done very well with 911SCs!

The 911SC was replaced in 1984 by the 3.2 Carrera which, to the untrained eye, is almost identical. And, to be honest, that's because it is virtually identical.

There's a clue to the major difference in the car's name – it had a 3.2-litre engine that produced 231bhp, but it's not such a free-revving unit as the SC's so some people, me included, prefer the feel of the 3.0-litre. That said, there's not much in it and the 3.2 is also a tough engine.

Initially, the Carrera 3.2 was offered with the same 915 gearbox as the SC, albeit with revised ratios to give more relaxed cruising (and better economy) in fourth and fifth gears. However, in 1987 the car was treated to the new Getrag G50 gearbox which offered smoother changes and a shorter, more modern-looking, gearlever. You can tell the difference between the 'boxes by the fact that on the G50 reverse is to the left and forwards, whereas on the 915 it's to the right and backwards. Today, these later cars are more sought after than the earlier 915-equipped models. However, don't dismiss the 915 gearbox – get a good one and it is a joy to use.

The Carrera 3.2 was phased out in 1989. Today, it's gained a reputation for being reliable and relatively affordable to own and run. For many years, the Carrera 3.2 was considered an ideal first foray into 911 ownership. Now, though, as with the SC, prices have risen and you're looking at least £35,000 to buy a reasonable example.

Don't be led into a false sense of security by the fact that SCs and Carrera 3.2s cars have fully galvanised bodyshells. The treatment slows down rust, but it certainly doesn't stop it. Furthermore, most cars will have had bodywork damage at some stage in their lives and, if that's not repaired properly, rust can quickly set in.

Remember, even the youngest of these 911s is almost 20 years old, so it's rare to find one that hasn't got at least some corrosion. And some have lots of rust. A rotten 911 can be very expensive to repair, so don't be tempted into buying a cheap one, thinking you can patch up the corrosion and make it look good. A few bubbles in the paintwork can hide untold horrors, especially in the complex sill construction.

You *Can* Drive a Porsche

964 Carrera 2 and 4

By the 1980s, the 911 was starting to look dated, and Porsche had to do something drastic. The result was the 964 of 1989.

First introduced as the Carrera 4, this car was radical in that it featured four-wheel-drive, although a rear-wheel-drive Carrera 2 followed. The engine was a 3.6-litre unit that pumped out a useful 250bhp via a refined version of the previous G50 five-speed gearbox.

The 964 kept the same basic 911 body shape, but it was updated with integrated deformable bumpers and a clever rear spoiler that lifted when the car reached 50mph, and then dropped down again at a little over walking pace, thus maintaining the clean, classic 911 looks.

Inside, the basic Porsche 911 cabin remained but it was updated with new trim, a better heating system and a shorter gearstick. Subtle changes that went a long way to making the 964 feel like a modern car.

You *Can* Drive a Porsche

Some early 964s had problems with engine oil leaks, so Porsche modified the engine to solve the problem. However, by then the car had developed a reputation for leaks and that stuck for many years. Hence, the 964 became an unwanted 911 and prices fell dramatically.

Today, people appreciate the 964 for what it is – a great car and a useful combination of classic and modern looks and technology. I've owned a couple myself and I love them. The only downside is that this new-found appreciation has meant that 964s are no longer cheap. Far from it, with prices starting at around £35,000 and rising to over £60,000 for good examples of the Carrera 2. They are more complex than the preceding 911SC and 3.2 Carrera, though, so be prepared for higher running costs. On the plus side, they're easier to live with on a day-to-day basis, if you find the earlier 911s too, well, old-fashioned.

The problem with Porsche 964s is finding a good one. Because they were once unloved and relatively inexpensive, many fell into the hands of people who can't afford to keep them properly maintained, so a depressing number are not great, with iffy service histories, scruffy interiors and leaky engines.

On the plus side, though, it's rare to find a really rusty 964 – if you do, walk away – and the cars are generally tough and fun to drive.

You *Can* Drive a Porsche

People often ask if they should go for a Carrera 2 or Carrera 4. Some say that the four-wheel-drive car suffers excessive understeer; I've owned one and, yes, there is more understeer than with a Carrera 2, but it's not a real problem. The four-wheel-drive gives better traction and handling, while the rear-drive car feels more like a classic 911 and is more fun on track. You will pay a premium for a Carrera 2 over a 4 because of its increased desirability and rarity.

You *Can* Drive a Porsche

993 Carrera 2 and Carrera 4

The 911 received its first major restyle in 1994 when the 993 range was introduced. With its curvaceous wings and swept-back headlamps this was hailed by many as the best 911 ever.

It's still considered so today by people who bemoan the passing of the air-cooled engine – the 993 was the last 911 to be so-equipped. It's also a well-sorted car – you could argue that Porsche had 30 years to get it right – with new, multi-link rear suspension that gives better ride and handling than before, a rock-solid engine and, for he first time, a six-speed gearbox.

The engine was a development of the 3.6-litre 964 unit but fitted with self-adjusting hydraulic tappets (which reduce servicing costs). Peak power was 272bhp – a useful 22bhp up on the 964. In 1995, for the 1996 model year, the 993 engine was uprated to 285bhp. This was achieved by the adoption of a new induction technology called Varioram – you'll find the word embossed on the inlet manifold on all but the first of these uprated engines.

You *Can* Drive a Porsche

Inside, the traditional 911 interior was tweaked but remained essentially unchanged, and is tough and hard-wearing, if a bit quirky.

The 993 also carried on the optional Tiptronic automatic gearbox of the 964 but, from 1994 this was renamed Tiptronic S and came with F1-style fingertip controls on the steering wheel.

Also new was the Targa. Out when the rather clumsy roll-hoop of previous Targas and in came a very neat glass roof panel that slid back under the rear window. The 993 Targa is relatively rare, but watch out for creaking roof panels.

Because the 993 is such a popular car, prices have remained firm, with the early, high-mileage examples starting at around £35,000. However, if you buy a good one (it's worth spending a bit more) you'll have a reliable, easy to live with and affordable 911 that will always attract admiring glances. Also, you're unlikely to lose any money when you come to sell – in fact, there's a fair chance it'll go up in value.

As with the 964, don't get too hung up on two- or four-wheel-drive, unless you're going to use the car on track, in which case the rear-drive Carrera 2 is more fun.

So a 993 really is a good buy. You get drop-dead gorgeous looks, plenty of power and good

You *Can* Drive a Porsche

handling, reliable mechanicals, traditional 911 build quality and excellent residuals.

You *Can* Drive a Porsche

996 Carrera and Carrera 4

All through the 911's history, up until 1998, you could trace its heritage right back to that first 911 of 1963. The problem was, though, that Porsche had pushed the envelope to the limit by the time the 993 came along in 1993. In 30 years the 911's engine power had risen from 130bhp to 300bhp, while the handling had gone from somewhat hairy to almost perfect.

Even so, customers were demanding ever more. Porsche knew that, with the 993's replacement, it would have to offer yet more power and that just wasn't feasible with the old air-cooled engine, particularly since ever-stricter noise and emissions regulations were being imposed by governments around the world.

The solution was to build an all-new car, codenamed 996. This had a 3.4-litre air-cooled engine and a larger bodyshell that gave more interior space. The 911 quirks, such as floor-mounted pedals and confusing dash controls, disappeared and in came a more conventional and modern interior.

You *Can* Drive a Porsche

It was a Porsche 911 that appealed to a wider market and it was an instant sales success. However, there were some occasional issues with the engine; there were tales of cylinder bores cracking and oil leaks from the rear main seal (RMS) where the crankshaft protrudes from the front of the engine, and intermediate shaft (IMS) bearing failure.

Porsche modified the design of the engine and replaced affected ones under warranty but, rather like with the 964, the damage was done. The 996 gained a reputation for being a risky buy – a replacement engine cost around £8000. So that, coupled with the fact there are plenty out there, has meant that these modern 911s are today surprisingly affordable, with early cars selling for as little as £12,000.

Another factor that affects value is that the 996 has not worn as well as older 911s – it doesn't have that same rock-solid build quality. Interiors, in particular, can soon look scruffy, while it's rare to find a 996 without small parking dents in the doors, which are made from thin steel.

So, should you buy one? Well, yes, I think you should. Serious engine failures are relatively rare – you just tend to hear about them via Internet forums – while RMS leaks, while common, tend to be annoying rather than anything else. The faulty seal can be inexpensively replaced at the same time as a clutch change.

Because the 996 is a relatively cheap 911, many have fallen into the hands of people who can't afford to maintain them (it's the old 964 story all over again), so there are some sadly neglected examples out there, that you should avoid. Seek out a car with a good service history that shows that it's been cherished by a caring and diligent owner, and steer clear of cars that have been updated with boy-racer accruements such as aftermarket wheels and bodykits.

In 2001, the 996 was heavily revised with, among other things, restyled headlamps, a tweaked interior and a larger 3.6-litre engine. These benefit from a bit more power and torque but the engine is a little less willing to rev, so you lose some of the fun associated with the original 3.4-litre version. On the whole, though, the additional refinement of the facelifted car (it has a glovebox, for instance) makes it a more attractive buy, with prices starting at around £15,000.

The one 996 Carrera that is holding its value better than most is the wide-bodied Carrera 4S. With Turbo styling and a full-width rear reflector (a welcome hark back to earlier 911s), it looks fantastic and the Turbo suspension and brakes make it a good drive, too. Prices have risen in the last couple of years and it's been flagged by many

You *Can* Drive a Porsche

as a future classic. You need at least £22,000 to buy into a Carrera 4S and its arguably too special to use every day.

Buy yourself a standard 996 Carrera or Carrera 4, though, and you will have a superb 911 that you really could use all year round. The 996 is the most affordable Porsche 911 you can buy and is also a great 911. You shouldn't go wrong if you start off with a good example.

You *Can* Drive a Porsche

997 Carrera and Carrera S

The 996-model 911 was criticised by some people for being bland-looking and lacking the essential 911 character. In reality, though, the 996 is an excellent 911 and it's hard to define what that missing character was, but Porsche's designers took the comments seriously when they were planning a successor.

The 997 came out in 2004 and is essentially a heavily revised 996 that draws on the 993's successful styling – inside and out – and is a thoroughly good-looking car that is great to drive.

In Carrera and Carrera 4 form, the 997 has a 3.6-litre engine that produces 325bhp, while the wider-bodied Carrera S and Carrera 4S have 355bhp 3.8-litre powerplants.

New to the 997 was Porsche Active Suspension Management (PASM). Standard on the S and optional on the Carrera, this intelligent system gives you the choice of two suspension settings – Normal and Sport, the latter being firmer and ideal for track use.

You *Can* Drive a Porsche

The 997 had an all-new interior with hints of the angular 993 cockpit. Most people prefer it to the 996's cabin but there are people – me included – that thought that the curvaceous and modern 996 dashboard complemented the car's exterior curves better. Sadly, the 997 interior tends not to wear well, with the leather on the seats particular vulnerable to scuffing.

Today, the 997 is a very affordable 911, which is not surprising when you consider that Porsche had built 100,000 of the things by 2007. Today, it is the most plentiful 911 on the second-hand market, far exceeding even 996 numbers. Prices start at under £20,000 for an early, high-mileage example but, as ever, it's worth spending a bit more to get a good one. Once you do, it should hold its value very nicely.

The later 997, referred to as the Gen2, had an all-new engine which doesn't suffer the (occasional) issues of the 996 and early 997 units. These cars, being newer, are more expensive and still have some depreciating to do, so aren't the best choice of a Clever Car Buyer. That said, they will still hold their value better than most £50,000 cars so, if you want a relatively modern Porsche, they're worth considering.

991 Carrera and Carrera S

In 2011, Porsche introduced the 991-model 911 which, for only the third time in the 911's life, was an all-new car. Bigger, more powerful, more efficient and more luxurious than before, the 991 is a remarkable feat of engineering but I can't help feeling that, in the strive for perfection, Porsche's engineers have dialled out some of the 911's quirky character.

More importantly for the purposes of this book, 991s are still too new to have stopped depreciating and so should be avoided by Clever Car Buyers. Sorry about that...

You *Can* Drive a Porsche

Pre-1979 classic 911s

'Classic' is a bit of a woolly term but it's a useful, if not strictly correct, way of describing 911s from the 1960s and 1970s.

I've chosen to bundle these Porsches (and there is a huge variety) together in this book, rather than detailing them separately. Why? Because they are generally quite specialised cars and you can easily get your fingers burnt.

Some cars from this period, such as the wonderful Carrera 2.7RS from 1973 are true collectors' items that are very sought-after and extremely expensive. If you've got the money and you know what you're doing, then one of these could certainly be a good investment. However, if you're in that sort of league, then I think it's safe to assume that you're somewhat beyond the readership of this book!

Other 911s from the 1960s and, especially, the 1970s sometimes come up for sale at temptingly low prices but be warned – there is usually a reason for a 911 being cheap.

And the most common reason is that these older 911s didn't have fully galvanised bodyshells and so they rust – badly. The dreaded tinworm can appear in all sorts of places; in particular in the front wings, the sills and around the rears of the door shuts. Often the corrosion may not look that bad on the surface, but don't be fooled – if you can see rust, the chances are there is much more hidden away in the complex bodyshell.

Rusty front wings can be unbolted and replaced, but new ones are expensive and you may find that there is also corrosion to the inner wings below that needs repairing. The sills are a tricky structure to fix and require specialist attention; again, once you start taking things apart, inevitably, more problems will appear.

So any bodywork repair can be very expensive, indeed, and that's before you come to repaint the restored shell. Oh, and don't be tempted to fill and paint over corrosion; not only will it bubble through in time, but you could also be compromising the car's rigidity and, therefore, safety.

On top of bodywork issues, cheap early 911s could also have mechanical problems. Don't believe anyone who tells you that a 911 engine is just like a Beetle's – it isn't. It's a complex machine that requires specialist skills and equipment to rebuild; it's not something most DIY mechanics

You *Can* Drive a Porsche

can tackle, and neither can jobbing mechanics. It needs someone skilled and familiar with 911s.

Now don't get me wrong, I love classic 911s. They look wonderful with their unsullied bodywork and non-no-nonsense interiors, and they are a joy to drive as well. They're just not an ideal choice for someone starting off on their 911 adventure. Keep those classic dreams for the future, when you've learnt more about the cars and have saved up some more money by being a Clever Car Buyer.

You *Can* Drive a Porsche

You *Can* Drive a Porsche

The RS, GT3 and GT2

Any 911 is a performance car, but Porsche has long offered versions that are designed for serious driving, on track or road.

The RS name first appeared on a production 911 in 1972. The now-legendary Carrera 2.7 RS achieved its performance advantage, partly through a more powerful engine, but mainly by being lighter in weight than its standard counterpart. Losing mass is an effective and economical way to improve, not only performance, but also handling.

The 2.7 RS is now a very sought after and valuable 911 and examples change hands for huge amounts of money. This has had an effect on later cars to carry the RS name, such as the 964 and 993 versions, with prices of these shooting up in recent years.

The 964 RS and 993 RS are both superb cars and a lot of fun to drive. Some people will tell you that they have a rock-hard ride quality, but they're really not that bad at all. Losing the weight and firming up the suspension has transformed the feel of them, and they drive quite differently to the standard Carreras on which they're based.

When Porsche produced a performance version of the 996, it came up with the GT3 which, despite a reduced specification, is actually heavier than the standard car, thanks to a very different engine. Again, though, it stands apart from the Carrera and is a lot of fun to drive. Porsche produced the original GT3 in limited numbers from 1999 to 2000, and then returned to the concept in 2003 with a full production model, usually known as the MkII.

There was also an RS version of the MkII, which was a lighter weight car. When launched, these were snapped up by speculators hoping that a new Porsche with an RS badge would be a sound investment. It took a while for this to happy but, today, these cars are valuable.

There was also a 997 GT3 and GT3 RS sold in 2007. Again, anything with an RS badge is sure to be sought after in the future.

The last car in this category is the GT2. Essentially, an extreme version of the 911 Turbo with rear-wheel-drive, the GT2 was first offered in 993 form. This was a wild car that needed to be treated with respect and has become a real collectors' item.

You *Can* Drive a Porsche

The 996 GT2 and 997 GT2 that followed have also gone on to become collectors's cars. They are more extreme and less usable than the Turbos on which they are based, but they do have rarity and excitement on their side.

You *Can* Drive a Porsche

What about a Turbo?

The word 'Turbo' is synonymous with Porsche and in particular with the 911. When Porsche first turbocharged the 911 back in 1974, it unwittingly produced an automotive icon. The original 911 Turbo, with its distinctive wide wheel arches and trademark rear spoiler, became a symbol of power and wealth.

Those first Turbos are a lot of fun to drive, but they can bite back – they suffer from serious turbo lag and all the power is going through the rear wheels only. Porsche gradually improved things and, with the launch of the 993 Turbo in 1996, finally sorted it.

Today, the 993 Turbo is one of the most coveted Porsches of all, and for good reason. Twin turbochargers, instead of a single one, reduce turbo lag, while the power goes through all four wheels. Oh, and just look at it! The combination of 993 lines, wider rear arches and that rear spoiler makes for a real visual feast.

You *Can* Drive a Porsche

The Turbo got even better with the 996 version. Widely hailed as the best car in the world, the 996 Turbo offered astonishing performance and handling – in fact, some said it was just too good to enjoy on public roads and it felt sterile to drive. The 997 Turbo moved things on even further but did manage to inject some soul back into the car.

For a while, the 996 Turbo really was a bargain supercar with prices starting at just £25,000, making it a great choice for a Clever Car Buyer. Sadly those days are long gone and you're looking at spending at least £10,000 for a reasonable example. Still a lot of car for the money and depreciation shouldn't be an issue. The same applies to the 997 Turbo but not yet to the newer 991 Turbo which will still drop in value.

Boxster

Developed in conjunction with the 996-model 911, the open-top Boxster was an entry-level model to replace the ageing 968.

The first Boxster of 1997 had a 2.5-litre engine mounted amidships. It was criticised for being underpowered, so Porsche increased the capacity to 2.7-litre in 1999 and also added the more powerful Boxster S with its 3.2-litre powerplant.

The Boxster was a great sales success, giving Porsche much-needed income to develop new models such as the Cayenne. There's no doubt that the Boxster is a fun car to drive, too – even the 2.5-litre version is OK if you drop the roof and enjoy the sunshine and superb handling.

I remember thinking, when the Boxster came out, that one day it would become a cheap Porsche, rather like the 944. And that day has arrived – you can pick up an early Boxster for less than £5000, making it the cheapest way to own a modern Porsche.

You *Can* Drive a Porsche

Sadly, though, the Boxster didn't inherit the hewn-from-granite build quality of the 944 and many early examples have become very rattley, which I find irritating when I'm driving. Find a good one, though, with a decent service history and you'll have a car that still looks expensive and should give you a lot of enjoyment.

If you can afford it, go for a later 2.7-litre model or even an S. Oddly, these 3.2-litre cars don't demand a premium on the second-hand market, maybe Boxster buyers are more into image than power, I don't know. Post-2001, the Boxster had a glass rear window instead of the plastic one of the original car which was vulnerable to damage.

If you're on a tight budget and want a Porsche you can enjoy every day, then you won't go far wrong with a Boxster.

Cayman

The Cayman is essentially a hard-top Boxster, which led to Jeremy Clarkson dubbing it the 'Coxster', which is rather unkind.

It's a lovely looking car, the Cayman – better looking than the Boxster in my eyes – and its lines draw on Porsche's heritage very well (it even has a 944-style hatchback).

Power comes from a 245bhp 2.7-litre engine, in the case of the standard car, and a 3.4-litre unit in the 295bhp Cayman S.

The Cayman is renowned for its handling prowess, thanks to its mid-engined layout, and the immediacy of the driving experience. Indeed, some say it's the spiritual successor to the original 911, arguing that the current 911 is too big and bloated. Personally, I disagree – as good as the Cayman is, it's not a rear-engined car and so doesn't feel like a 911.

It is, though, less expensive than a 911 to buy new and so has found many fans; people wanting more something more macho than a Boxster and a purer sports car.

Today, early Caymans are great value for money, but tend to hold their value better than the rather more common Boxsters. The starting price is around £14,000 and for that you get a fantastic car that will give you a lot of fun. In fact, every time I drive a Cayman, part of me wonders why anyone would want a 911. They really are that good.

Cayenne

The Cayenne was a huge (in more ways than one) departure for Porsche when it appeared in 2002. What was a sports car company doing making an off-roader? Expanding its markets and, therefore, its profits, that's what.

There's no doubt that the Cayenne is an impressive bit of kit – not only is it a capable off-roader, it also has good on-road manners with real Porsche-like performance, coupled with a spacious and luxurious interior.

Three basic variants were offered. First came the entry-level 250bhp V6, then the V8-powered Cayenne S that produced 340bhp, and finally the range-topping and outrageous Turbo with its 450bhp engine that propelled the big car to 62mph in just 5.6 seconds and on to a top speed of 165mph which, quite frankly, is just crazy for a car that size!

Because Porsche developed the Cayenne as a high-performance car, it refused to offer a diesel-powered version until later. Which means that all earlier Cayennes are thirsty petrol drinkers and expensive to run. And that, of course, leads to heavy depreciation – buyers of new Cayennes may be able to afford to run them, but other people can't, so there is not a high demand for them second-hand.

And that's great news if you fancy a Cayenne because you can pick an acceptable early one up for as little as £7,000. That's a whole lot of car for the money, but brace yourself for heavy fuel bills, especially if you choose a Turbo.

944 and 968

The entry-level 944 debuted in 1984 and followed on from the 924. However, the new car had muscular wheelarch extensions and a more powerful 2.5-litre engine.

I've always liked the 944 – it's a good, solid car to drive and is practical, too, with its large glass rear hatch.

They are today affordable modern classics, with tired and scruffy early 944 Lux examples going for less than £3000.

However, the later 944 S2 with its 3.0-litre engine and revised interior is a much nicer car and worth considering. Prices have gone up in recent years, though, so 944s aren't the bargains they once were. You need to be spending upwards of £9000 for an S2 now.

Be careful, though – many 944s out there have been bought as cheap cars by people who can't afford to maintain them and a neglected 944 engine can suffer expensive problems. So don't buy the cheapest you find but hang on until you find one that's been looked after by a true Porsche enthusiast – you still won't have to pay a lot of money for it.

The 968 is essentially a revised 944 with new front and rear ends, more power and a six-speed gearbox. The 968's looks have stood the test of time better and not that many were built, so it has rarity on its side, all of which means prices have remained firm and, recently, have increased. You can still buy one for around £12,000 though.

Particularly sought after is the Club Sport which, with its stripped out interior and firm suspension, has proved to be a great trackday weapon. Club Sport prices have almost doubled in recent years, with prices starting at £30,000

You may also come across the 968 Sport – a UK-only model that has the Club Sport suspension but all the luxuries (electric windows and so on) of the standard car, which makes it a good compromise. Expect to pay upwards of £18,000 for a Sport.

928

The Porsche 928 dates right back to 1978 and it was developed to replace the 911, but it never did. It was an entirely different car, with a water-cooled V8 mounted at the front, driving the back wheels via a rear-mounted gearbox.

The 928 was a large car and boasted spaceship-like lines that seemed very futuristic in the mid-1970s, with exposed pop-up headlamps and lots of glass, including a lifting hatchback.

It was the same story inside, with a luxurious and modern interior with plenty of space for two adults to stretch out and enjoy long journeys, and seats for kids in the back

Over the years, the 928 evolved into the last and best version – the GTS of 1992. This had a 5.3-litre, 32-valve V8 engine that produced 350bhp (by contrast, the first 928 had 240bhp). With a 0-60mph time of 5.6 seconds and a top speed of 171mph, this truly was a supercar. Also, unlike most earlier 928s, the GTS had a five-speed manual gearbox, not an automatic, to make the best use of the power, while the suspension was firmer to improve the handling.

The 928 was quietly discontinued in 1995, while the 911 has gone from strength to strength. However, the 928 – especially in GTS guise – was a great car in its own right, and its space-age lines still look modern today.

But should you buy one? Well, if you like the feel of a large V8 and want a long-distance cruiser rather than an out-and-out sports car, then a 928 offers good value for money but you should definitely avoid cheap 'projects' as they'll turn into money pits.

Do try to buy from a true Porsche enthusiast, though; someone who's cherished the car and had it properly maintained. And be aware that your fuel bill won't be small. The most affordable Porsche

You may be reading this book thinking it's all very well suggesting buying a Porsche for £15,000 or less, but you can't afford that. Maybe you're in a low-paid job, have a crippling mortgage and a baby on the way.

Not to worry, there's a classic Porsche out there you can buy for under £5000.

I'm taking about the 924; a model introduced in 1976 and which went on to be a great sales success, perhaps even saving Porsche from bankruptcy. It was an entry-level model but still an expensive car; think of it as the Boxster of its day.

The 924 was never a fast car, with its 2.0-litre engine producing a modest 125bhp but it was, as you'd expect from Porsche, a well-built machine. It also handled nicely, thanks to a near 50/50 weight distribution due to its front-mounted engine and rear-mounted gearbox.

I once owned a 924 and found it was a great car. It looked superb, with clean, uncluttered lines, it felt solid and sophisticated and stuck to the road like a limpet. OK, it could have done with more power, but it was fun nonetheless, and its large opening rear hatch gave plenty of luggage space – I remember carrying my mountain bike in mine! I was only young at the time, but I felt a million dollars driving around in my first Porsche.

That is great news for Porsche buyers on a budget. There's more good news, too. Although 924s were once two-a-penny on the second-hand market, today there are precious few left and prices are starting to rise. Buy a reasonable example today and it can only appreciate in value.

Do bear in mind that a 924 at a rock-bottom price is unlikely to be a great car; the chances are the mileage will be enormous and the bodywork and interior will be scruffy. The engines are fundamentally tough, though, and if it's running reasonably well, it's safe to assume that it will continue to do so; at least for a while.

The best policy with an ultra-cheap Porsche like this is not to pour money into it. OK, tidy up the bodywork and interior (it's amazing what a good polish and vacuum can do) and have any minor jobs done to keep the car running safely, but if anything expensive goes wrong, then the best solution is simply to shrug your shoulders and take the Porsche to the scrapyard. After all, you can always find another one.

When you're looking for 924s, you'll probably come across three versions; the 924 Lux, 924S and 924 Turbo. The Lux was the standard 2-litre car sold in the UK from 1976 to 1985 and that's what you're most likely to be getting for bargain-basement money.

The 924S was in production from 1985 to 1988 and was basically the same car as the 924 but with a larger, 2.5-litre engine that produced 150bhp (uprated to 160bhp for later cars). In fact, the engine was a downrated version of that used in the 944 and really did a lot to transform the performance and refinement of the car. These are now going up in value more than the original version.

The 924 Turbo is an interesting beast made from 1979 to 1983. As the name suggests, it's a

924 with a turbocharged engine that produced 170bhp (177bhp from 1980); a useful increase over the standard car's modest output. A rare car now (there are believed to be only around 60 left in the UK) these are now very sought after, with prices touching £20,000.

Finally, occasionally you'll see a 924 Carrera GT, a very rare car that was a more powerful version of the 924 Turbo and recognisable by large wheelarch extensions (which later formed the inspiration for the 944's arches). A real collectors' item, you can pay a lot of money for one – but you'll be able to tell your friends that you drive a Carrera GT, the name given to Porsche's more recent supercar!

You *Can* Drive a Porsche

You *Can* Drive a Porsche

How to buy a Porsche

Buying the right car is the key to a happy start in Porsche ownership that will give you pleasure for years to come. Buy the wrong car, though, and you'll end up spending money, not enjoying the car and becoming thoroughly disillusioned before going back to a Mondeo. Not the way forward for a Clever Car Buyer.

So how to buy the right Porsche? By taking your time and doing your homework, that's how. First of all, you need to decide just what model of Porsche you want. This book gives you a general overview of what's available, but I do recommend that you go along to a dealer and have a good look at and drive some different ones. A 993, for instance, is a very different animal to a 996 – you need to decide what is right for you.

It may sound corny, but join a Porsche club and get to meet some of the local members. Look at their cars, get them to take you out in them, and ask them for advice. Porsche owners are generally very friendly and love nothing better than to talk about their cars.

You *Can* Drive a Porsche

Once you've decided what model you want, you can start to paint a picture in your mind about what your perfect Porsche will look like. Think about colour – what shades do you like and which do you hate? And what about interiors? Does red leather do it for you, or do you prefer black or grey? How about options? Is a sunroof important? Do you need air-conditioning (rare on pre-1990s Porsches in the UK)? Is an automatic gearbox your thing, or would you prefer a manual?

Once you've created an image of your perfect Porsche, you now need to destroy it. Well, not exactly, but you should be flexible when buying used. Sure, you may love grey paintwork but it would be silly to turn down an excellent car at the right price just because it's finished in black. Also, black leather may be your first choice, but perhaps dark blue would do. Decide what you will compromise on and what is a must or a no-no. The more flexible you can be, the more cars you will be able to choose from, making it quicker and easier to find a good example.

Oh, and don't forget to set a budget at this time. Again, you should be reasonably flexible here, too. So if you have, say, £20,000 to spend on a car, it would be good to know if you could stretch to £22,000 if you really had to. Do make sure, though, that you don't overstretch yourself – you need to have some money in reserve for running and maintaining the car.

I could say that now, and only now, is the time to start looking for a Porsche, but the chances are you've already been dipping into the classifieds, and that's actually a good idea – it helps you to get a feel for what is out there and what prices people are asking. These days, the Internet is the best place to look for used Porsches and Pistonheads is my favourite place to search. The site works so well – you can enter your search criteria, including model, age, price, mileage and so on, so you don't have to waste time trawling through loads of unsuitable adverts.

Pistonheads also lets you specify the search area, based on distance from your home (you're asked to enter your postcode). Now, if I were buying, say, a Ford Focus, I'd limit the search to within 40 miles, knowing that there will be plenty of suitable cars nearby. Porsches, though, are much rarer animals so you need to spread the net further afield – in the UK I usually specify a nationwide search, it's worth travelling to get the right car.

Should you buy privately or from a dealer? That's a tricky question to answer because there are pros and cons to both options. If you're choosing a dealer, go to one that specialises in Porsches; I'm wary of used car salesmen, who just happen to have a Porsche slipped in between

You *Can* Drive a Porsche

rows of Mondeos and Primeras, because they won't know much about the car. That means that, not only will they be unable to advise you properly, they may not even know if it's any good or not.

A reputable Porsche specialist, on the other hand, is unlikely to have taken on a dud car, because they have a reputation to uphold and know what they're looking for when they take on cars. They'll also have a selection of Porsches to choose from and will offer a warranty.

I hate to generalise, but if you're spending £30,000 or more on a Porsche, I'd recommend going to a specialist dealer rather than buying one privately or from a general car trader. If you're spending that sort of money, there is peace of mind to be had by purchasing from someone with premises, service facilities and warranties.

The downside to buying from a dealer is that you usually spend more for the car – the dealer, quite reasonably, needs to make a profit and he has premises and other expenses to cover; not to mention the warranty. That's why privately sold cars tend to be cheaper.

Buying privately can, then, save you money so long as you are careful. Always arrange to view a car at the seller's home – not at a remote car park somewhere, and ask to go into the house to use the toilet, say, so you can be sure it really is his or her home. You should also check that the address tallies with that on the registration document. Talk to the seller and find out how long they have owned the car and how much they know about it. If they seem vague, then be suspicious. A real enthusiast should be happy to chat about his or her Porsche.

Whether the car is being sold by a dealer or a private owner, the first thing to look at is its service history. Porsches demand to be well-maintained and a car with an incomplete service history will be worth less, especially in the UK. There should be a service book (usually in a leather wallet) in the glovebox that is stamped by the garage each time that a service is completed.

For the first few years of a Porsche's life, this is usually done by an Official Porsche Centre (OPC) but they are expensive so most cars drop out of the official dealer network after four or five years. If a car has continued to have been maintained by an OPC, that's good news because it's a sign of a caring, fastidious owner – if they were happy to have spent top-money on servicing, they are unlikely to have skimped in other areas.

Don't worry, though, if you find stamps that aren't from an OPC – that's quite normal. What you do want to see, mind, is the name of a known Porsche specialist, not some backstreet garage. Look at adverts a Porsche magazine, for instance, or ask members of a Porsche Internet forum if a garage is reputable.

Service stamps don't tell the full story, though. A car could have had a basic service but the garage may have come up with a list of advisory faults that the owner may not have bothered to have had put right – especially if he was about to sell the car. So I always like to see a good supply of receipts to back up the history – preferably neatly filed. These are invaluable for building up a detailed picture of a car's history. Look for evidence of major jobs, such as a clutch change or an engine rebuild, which is always good news. However, also check for receipts for small items – these show that an owner has been really particular. I remember seeing one 911 where the owner had had it checked by an OPC and had then gone through the list of minor faults, putting them right one by one. He'd even replaced the cigarette lighter because it didn't work – not that he smoked, he just wanted everything perfect. That's a sign of a pampered Porsche.

Other encouraging signs include a heated and tiled garage (surprisingly common for even modestly priced Porsches.), Zymöl or similar high-priced polish (I can't see the point myself, but it's amazing what people spend on valeting products) and a general enthusiasm for Porsche from the seller. A conscientious seller will sometimes service and MoT the car before putting it on the market, even if one isn't due – another good sign.

It's also nice to see old MoT certificates – not only do they suggest that the owner has been fastidious with the history, but they are also a useful way of verifying that the mileage is correct – the mileage at the time of the test is recorded on each certificate. Also, I don't like to see a car whose MoT is about to expire – why hasn't the seller bothered to renew it?

When I'm viewing a Porsche, I go through all the paperwork before I even look at the car itself. I also like to chat with the owner to get an idea about them – why are they selling the car? Are they buying another Porsche? It's always nice if the seller turns out to be a real enthusiast.

Now it's time to check out the car itself. There isn't room in this book to go into great detail about what to look for on each particular model of Porsche, but there are some things that are common to all that it's worth checking.

I usually begin by going over the bodywork, looking for dents, chips and evidence of damaged or repaired panels. It's not unusual for front bumpers and bonnets to have been resprayed – they are susceptible to chips – but the work should have been done to such a high standard that you're hard-pressed to tell it's not the original finish. Cheap paint jobs suffer from runs, a matt finish, bubbling, overspray on adjacent panels and trim, and orange peel – a textured finish like the skin of the fruit.

I'm always wary of a Porsche that's had a full respray and will inspect it extra carefully. Why has the work been done? It may be simply because the old paint was getting tired (not unusual on older cars but no excuse on a newer model) but it could also be because of major accident damage. Ask questions and look for a receipt for the work in the history file. It's rare to find a Porsche that's been resprayed in a different colour to the original because it's expensive to do it properly, inside and out. If you come across a car that's a different colour in the boot and engine bay, walk away.

All Porsches can rust, despite the fact that they have had fully galvanised bodyshells for many years. Galvanising slows down the corrosion process, it doesn't stop it, so you'll be lucky to find a 25-year old Porsche without any rust somewhere. Rust, especially on a 911, can be expensive to put right, so tread carefully; what may look like a few bubbles in the paintwork could be evidence of more trouble underneath. Equally, if a car looks too good for its age, check carefully for evidence of swiftly-repaired rust patches.

Alloy wheels can become scuffed and corroded, so check these, too. Slight damage can be repaired, but big chunks knocked out of a rim can be trouble to put right. Remember, most alloy wheels are painted and lacquered and the finish has a limited lifespan before it needs refinishing. I like to see the original Porsche wheels on a car, but it's not unusual to see aftermarket rims, or ones from a later Porsche. This is fine, so long as they fit correctly.

Porsches are high-performance cars, so tyres should be a high-quality, well-known brand – remember that they are the only contact between you and a road – so look for names like Pirelli, Goodyear or Dunlop. Budget tyres from some unknown far-eastern company may not be suitable for high-speed use (which can invalidate your insurance), and also suggest that the owner has not been prepared to spend money on the car – what else have they skimped on?

While you're by the wheels, peek through the spokes and look at the brake discs – they should have a smooth, shiny surface (unless it's a recent Porsche with ceramic discs – look for yellow calipers). If they are heavily grooved, rusty, or have a deep ridge around the edge, they'll need replacing. The brake pads are harder to see, but they should each be at least 5mm thick.

Inside, Porsches built before around 1997 usually have tough, hard-wearing interiors. However, seats inevitably wear with age, especially around the side-bolsters, and carpets can become threadbare. Watch out for bodged wiring for aftermarket stereos, phone kits and so on. More modern Porsches, such as 996s, 997s and Boxsters have not stood the test of time (and mileage) so well inside, and trim can often become loose and rattley.

Mechanically, look for oil leaks from the engine and gearbox. A small amount of oil may not be serious but should be investigated further. It's worth sneaking a look at the vendor's garage floor for evidence of oil drips.

Ideally, you should view a car when its engine is cold, then you can see how easily it starts and how quickly it settles to a smooth idle. Because of their configuration, it's not unusual for 911 (and Boxster) engines to have smoky exhausts when first started – that's because oil seeps into the cylinders and then burns away when the engine runs, especially on high mileage examples. This is not a major concern so long as the smoke clears after the car's been driven a mile or so. If it doesn't clear, there's a fair chance the engine is in a bad way and requires expensive maintenance.

Only test-drive the Porsche if you are insured and the vendor is happy for you to do so. Usually, your own insurance policy only gives third-party cover, so if you damage the car you will be liable for any repairs.

You *Can* Drive a Porsche

On a test drive, check for the usual things you would look at when buying any car. Everything should work properly and there should be few squeaks, rattles or knocks. The clutch pedal should be smooth and relatively light – don't believe anyone who tells you Porsches have heavy clutches; that's a sign that the clutch mechanism is in trouble. You should be able to change gears smoothly and without graunching. Pre-1988 911s have what is called a 915 gearbox which requires gentle changes – if gears have been forced the 'box becomes damaged and you are unable to make smooth changes.

Next, make sure all the electrics, such as lights, electric windows, sunroof, remote locking and so on all work as they should.

If you like the car and it stands up to close scrutiny, then the next thing is to have it inspected by someone who knows Porsches inside out. There are two reasons for this. First, because they will have more experience of what to look for and will be better able to judge whether or not it's a good car. And second, it's very easy to put on rose-tinted spectacles in the excitement of buying your first Porsche – an independent specialist will be able to step back and give an impartial judgement. It's £300 or so very well spent.

If the inspection checks out, then you should get an HPI check done on the car to ensure that it is

You *Can* Drive a Porsche

not an insurance write-off, stolen or has some other dodgy history.

Finally, then, you are ready to buy your first Porsche!

You *Can* Drive a Porsche

Buying brand-new

Buying a brand-new Porsche would be nice, wouldn't it? You'd get to choose just the colour and specification you want. You'd drink coffee and eat little cakes in a swish showroom and would be fussed over by a salesman in a nice suit.

And just imagine going to collect your new car. There it would be, sitting gleaming and spotless outside the showroom. You'd shake the salesman's hand as he handed you the key and then get into the virgin driver's seat (is that a good description?) and drive off, knowing that no one has ever abused or damaged your shiny pride and joy. Perfect!

Well, it would be perfect if you could afford to cope with the depreciation. Now, to be fair, Porsches don't lose money anywhere near as fast as most prestige cars but look at some figures. A new 911 Carrera will cost you in the region of £76,000 in standard spec, but after four years, you'd be looking at selling it for about £40,000 – a £36,000 loss. Not something a Clever Car Buyer would be proud of.

You *Can* Drive a Porsche

However, that's mild compared to a new 911 Turbo at a hefty £126,000. After four years that would have almost halved in value to about £70,000. Not many people can afford to lose over £50,000 on a car, can they?

And those figures are for standard cars – no one buys a Porsche without adding some optional extras, and even metallic paint will cost you about £800. It's all too easy to increase the purchase price by £10,000 by ticking options – money you won't get back when it's time to sell.

Of course, not many people buy Porsches with hard cash – most opt for some sort of finance deal. Not only does this allow you to drive a car that you wouldn't otherwise be able to afford, there are tax and VAT advantages if you are buying the car through a company. It's worth taking advice from your accountant if that's the case.

Remember, though, that whatever you do, it's still going to cost you. It is argued that all you are doing on some of these finance deals is paying the cost of the interest on the money and the depreciation on the car – for a new 911 that would typically be about £1000 a month. So, again, you have to ask yourself if you can afford to lose that amount of money. If you can, then that's great – go for it. As I said, it would be lovely to own a brand-new Porsche.

You *Can* Drive a Porsche

Of course, newness is a novelty that wears off as soon as you drive the car. Inevitably, your Porsche is going to get dirty, scratched and chipped (show me a 911 without stonechips at the front), and the carpets will get grubby with muddy footprints. If you take pride in your cars (and you shouldn't be buying a Porsche if you don't) then surely you're better off buying a slightly used example. That way, you'll get less stressed about every little mark

You *Can* Drive a Porsche

How to sell a Porsche

Clever Car Buyers are also Clever Car Sellers. They want to make sure they lose as little money as possible between buying a car and selling it. In fact, the really smart guys actually make money on the deal – something that is entirely possible with Porsches, so long as you buy right and sell right.

The selling process should start the day you buy your Porsche. Read the chapter on buying and you'll see how important it is purchase from a caring and fastidious owner. Now that person is you – the better you care for your Porsche, the easier it will be to sell it on for top money. You could argue that the chapter on buying tells you all you need to know about selling.

It goes without saying that you should keep your Porsche in first-rate condition, so look after it. Keep it tucked up in a garage, if possible, polish it regularly, park it away from other vehicles in car parks and generally pamper it.

The chances are, the car wasn't perfect when you bought it, so spend time putting any faults right. It doesn't cost much to get minor dents and scratches removed by a specialist, for instance. Inside, leather can be treated with special cream to revitalise it, while a good-quality set of floor mats will freshen up a tired cockpit.

Don't make the mistake, mind, of doing all this just before you sell the car. What's the point of spending time and money on improving your car if you're not going to benefit from it? It's much better to get your Porsche in tip-top condition early on so you can enjoy it during your ownership.

Service history is critical to a Porsche's value and desirability, so don't skimp. Take the car to a well-known Porsche specialist (Official Porsche Centres are expensive so few owners of older models use them but there are plenty of good independents) and make sure that you keep all your receipts for work done and check that the service book is stamped and dated. Invest in a smart ring-binder and some plastic sleeves so you can keep all the paperwork in date order – not only will it make your life easier, potential buyers will be suitably impressed.

Inevitably, when you get your Porsche serviced, the technician will pick up on additional jobs that need doing, either immediately or in the near future – perhaps new brake pads and discs, or maybe an oil leak that needs seeing to. It can be tempting not to have such work done, especially if you're about to sell the car. However, if you don't astute buyers will see that you have neglected the car and will either walk away, or try to beat you down on price.

Tyres are another giveaway. A set of good-quality tyres for a Porsche is not cheap and it can be tempting to leave the old ones on or buy a set of budget boots. Again, though, neither option will put you in a potential buyer's good books.

The aim is to have a car that is close to perfect; one that has clearly been well maintained regardless of cost, and one that a new owner will immediately be able to enjoy without having to have anything done to it.

Buying a Porsche is also an emotional judgement, so you want a car that looks drop-dead gorgeous so a buyer just has to buy it, regardless of price. That means making sure that it is clean and shiny inside and out. And that typically means spending the best part of a weekend cleaning and polishing. Don't forget to clean under the wheelarches, in the boot and engine bay, under the seats and so on. The windows, too, should be spotless inside and out – something that makes a remarkable difference to a car's appearance. Whatever you do, though, don't be tempted to use shiny finishes on the tyres and dash – that just smacks of cheap second-hand car dealer, as if you're trying too hard. The car should be clean but not tarted up.

If you don't have the time or patience to clean your Porsche to this standard, then pay a professional valeter to do it. You'll be impressed by the results.

Once you've got the car up to standard, then is the time to start marketing it, and here the Internet is your weapon of choice. Auto Trader and Pistonheads are popular places to go when searching for Porsches, so get adverts on those sites. There are also various other websites and forums that offer Porsche classified adverts, so search those out, too.

Photographs of the car on the advert are essential and it's worth spending some time taking good ones. Don't photograph it in your driveway (unless, that is, you have a sweeping gravel drive with a country house behind.). Choose a bright (but not too sunny) day and drive off to a local beauty spot, or somewhere with a plain, simple background. Using a decent digital camera, shoot a selection of pictures of the car from various angles, as well as the interior and engine bay. If the car has a particularly impressive service record, lay out all the paperwork on the bonnet and take a photo of that as well. The photographs don't need to be fancy or arty, but should show the car clearly and pleasantly

You *Can* Drive a Porsche

Think carefully how you word your advert; it should be informative, honest and upbeat. Don't mislead people – if the car isn't in perfect condition, don't suggest that it is. Anyone who is interested in the Porsche will come and view it, so you may as well be honest from the start. However, do point out the positive things, such as service history, new items such as clutch or brakes (don't list little things such as a new battery, though – you're selling a Porsche, not an old Fiesta). Describe the car, giving the information you'd want to know if you were buying; the full and correct model name (eg. 996 Carrera Tiptronic); colour (the proper Porsche name, not just 'blue' or 'grey'); interior colour (again, use the correct term); significant options (sunroof, sports seats, sat-nav and so on); and any non-standard extras such as different wheels.

The whole point of the advert is to get people interested enough in the car to want to come and see it in preference to the many other Porsches they will have found online.

Always put a price on your advert. It can be hard to come up with a value for your car, but you need to be realistic; overprice it and you'll get no enquiries. The best thing to do is to start trawling the classified for a couple of weeks before you want to sell, so you can get a feel for the market and see what other people are asking. Do, though,

You *Can* Drive a Porsche

make sure you differentiate between trade and private sellers – the former will command higher prices than you will be able to achieve.

If all the above sounds like hassle, don't be tempted to throw the towel in and get a dealer to take the car in part-exchange for a new one. You're not going to realise the best price for your Porsche by doing that and it's really not the way Clever Car Buyers work. If you don't want the hassle of selling it yourself, find someone who will sell on your behalf, on a commission basis.

You *Can* Drive a Porsche

What about the environment?

Here's a fanciful story for you. Far, far away, on the planet Gerg, there's an environmental disaster going on. Why? Because people get bored with their homes very quickly and, every couple of years, they move to a brand-new one. Their old houses plummet in value and so get snapped up by less wealthy people but, soon, they too move away, wanting the prestige of a new house with the latest fashions in soft furnishings. So the old houses, most of which are perfectly good, become worthless and get bulldozed away to make room for new ones.

The house-builders are, of course, making a fortune and have realised that they don't have to build their houses very well because they don't need to last more than a few years.

The problem with all this is that the planet's precious resources are being depleted because raw materials are required to build the houses, and massive amounts of energy is consumed, in mining raw materials, transporting it to building sites and by the machines used for building (much of the house building is mechanised to save labour costs). Furthermore, more energy is wasted in knocking down the old houses and disposing of the waste.

The world's governments are concerned by this use of energy and so has passed draconian laws to force homes to be more environmentally friendly and so use less fuel for heating and lighting. This, of course, has the effect of encouraging people to move into the newer, cheaper to run homes, thus leading to a whole new cycle of house building, with its associated wastage.

In the midst of all this, there is a hardcore of inhabitants of Gerg who buck the trend and live in houses that were built some years back, before the obsession with new homes began. These period homes are solidly built and quite charming to look at and to live in. Indeed, they're looked upon as being prestigious and only for the wealthy because you occasionally have to employ artisans called plumbers and roofers to keep the houses in good order. And, of course, they cost more to heat and light, which means that the ever-growing environmental pressure groups demand that these lovely old homes be knocked down and replaced with new ones that use less energy. What they don't realise, though, is that the resources employed in doing that are far greater than just leaving the old dwelling there.

You *Can* Drive a Porsche

The people who live in these period houses are, naturally, very smug in the knowledge that their homes hold their value much better than the new, less well-built ones, and they don't have to worry about finding the money to move every few years. Sure, they have to seek out a craftsman to fix their toilet every once in a while, but that's no hardship in the great scheme of things, especially as they know that their lovely old homes are less damaging to the environment than the cheaply-built new ones that are springing up all over the place. If only more people could see the sense in not moving, but it's hard not to when the government and environmental groups are making people feel guilty for living in older houses. Maybe, just maybe, the inhabitants of Gerg will come to their senses and put a stop to all this

Of course, the above story is pure fiction but it's making an important point. On Gerg, it was houses that had become disposable and old ones were considered environmentally damaging. On Earth, we have exactly the same situation with cars. They have become disposable consumer items that are considered worthless before they are ten years old, even if they still have plenty of life left in them.

Why is this? Well, it's partly fashion and status; people want to be seen in the latest model of car and a new car is a symbol of wealth and success, even if it is just a bog-standard saloon. Car manufacturers are only too aware of this, which is why they produce face-lift models every year, to ensure that the new version stands out from the previous model; it's called planned obsolescence and is a powerful marketing tool, whether it's applied to cars, televisions or clothes.

What's more, the world's car manufacturers have made it increasingly easy to buy a new car, with attractive finance deals that allow you to drive off in the latest model for an attractive monthly payment. The catch is, though, that most of these rely on you paying a lump sum at the end of the deal which, invariably, involves trading in your existing (and perfectly good) car for a brand new one from the same manufacturer, ensuring that you're stuck with that brand until you can bear to break the cycle.

In other words, the car – like many other consumer items – has become a throwaway product. Once upon a time people used to repair things – whether it be kettles, televisions or socks – but these days, the chances are they'll chuck a broken item out and buy a new one. Even if you wanted to repair, say, a kettle, you'd struggle to find anyone willing to do it and, besides, it's usually cheaper to buy a shiny new one which will look great in your kitchen.

Cars are the same. OK, you will have minor problems fixed but, once your everyday saloon car has reached six or seven years old, you'd have to think very carefully before putting money into expensive repairs, such as an engine rebuild, because the car simply wouldn't be worth it – the cost of the repair would be greater than the value of the car and you'd be putting good money after bad. Far better to have it towed away to the scrapyard and then head off to the showroom to pick a shiny new model.

So the world's landfill sites are becoming clogged with consumer items that people don't want, either because they're not the latest model, or because they can't be bothered to repair them. And cars are one of the main offenders. OK, some components are recycled but even doing that uses up valuable energy.

And it's not only the old cars that are causing a problem; for every car scrapped a new one has to be built to replace it, and building cars uses a huge amount of energy; the raw materials have to be mined, refined and transported. A modern car is produced with thousands of components, many of which are manufactured in factories (all using energy) away from the main car plant, so parts then have to be transported, often great distances, before the vehicle can be assembled.

Then the factory that builds the car itself uses huge amounts of energy to run the assembly line and its associated machinery and, of course, the workers all have to travel to work; usually by car.

Finally, the finished car has to be transported to its place of sale; often to another country, so yet more energy is used. And, within just a few years, its life will be over.

Surely it would make far more sense to build cars that would last for longer and could be repaired indefinitely, a bit like we do with our homes? Of course it would – but cars would cost a lot more and manufacturers would lose all those lovely repeat sales. Besides, most of the population has been brainwashed into believing that new is best, so they're not going to pay extra for something that they won't want to keep more than a few years, will they?

Once upon a time, cars were built to last and there was a thriving industry of mechanics and welders to help you keep your Austin Seven or Morris Eight on the road, while many owners enthusiastically did their own maintenance; they'd no choice, they didn't have the means to buy a new car.

It was perhaps Ford that realised that cars could become fashion items. It was in the USA in the 1950s that the concept of a 'new' model every year began, with manufacturers changing the styling of radiator grilles and rear fins to ensure that people would know if you were driving last year's or this year's car.

The Ford Cortina was one of the first cars to bring this idea to the UK and it went down a storm, especially with company car drivers, for whom status was everything; it soon became a source of embarrassment not to have the latest model in the office car park. And the adoption of age-related numberplates in the UK from 1963 fuelled the desire to own the latest model yet more.

Car manufacturers followed the direction of white-good (fridges, washing machines and the like) makers and made their products as cheap to build as possible so that they could be more competitive in the marketplace while, at the same time, maximising profits. After all, what was the point of making cars tough and durable if buyers didn't want that?

Some manufacturers bucked the trend and continued to built high-quality cars that could go on for years and years – Volvo and Mercedes being notable examples – but they eventually realised that, if they were to survive, they would have to compete with other manufacturers and cut corners to keep costs down.

Even Porsche hasn't escaped. Compare a 911 from the 1980s to one from the late 1990s and the chances are that the newer car has not stood the test of time as well, while the older one feels so much more solid and over-engineered. To be fair to Porsche, the very latest models certainly feel more solid but I doubt that they will stand up to the test of time as well as the older ones.

Anyway, going back to those Ford Cortinas, when did you last see a Cortina on the road? Any model, from 1963 to 1982? Come to think of it, when did you last see an example of its successor, the jelly-mould Sierra of 1982 to 1993, driving around? And that car was replaced by the Mondeo Mk1 which today has also become a rare sight on our roads.

Actually, if you do see a Cortina and you're of a certain age, you may look at it with curiosity and nostalgia but if you spot a Sierra or early Mondeo, the chances are you'll view it with scorn, for the simple reason you've been conditioned to believe that old cars are rubbish and you've been exposed to Ford's newer models which have been carefully styled to make their predecessors look out-dated. It's all clever stuff.

In contrast, you're far more likely to see an old Porsche from the 1960s, 1970s or 1980s on the road, even though they were built in far fewer numbers than were Cortinas and Sierras. And here's a thing – you will never, ever, look at a 911 and think that it's rubbish. Sure, you'll realise that

You *Can* Drive a Porsche

it's old but that adds to its charm; an early 911 is a classic car and a joy to behold.

The reason you're more likely to see an old Porsche than an old Ford is that over 60 percent of Porsches built are still on the road today. That's an astonishing number; even more so when you consider that some will, inevitably, have been destroyed in accidents and it includes all Porsches right back to the 1950s, including the less undesirable 924 and 944, many of which have now, sadly, been scrapped because they ended up having very little value.

So what is it about Porsches that makes them last so well? They were very well built – especially the older cars. In fact, they're totally over-engineered in many areas, rather than built to a budget, which is excellent news when it comes to longevity. Start to take an air-cooled 911 to pieces and you'll what I mean. Even the fastenings for the door trim is over the top for what it's intended to do, but then at least it's not going to break on you, and it's easy to take off and put back.

This means that it's relatively simple to maintain a Porsche and there is a healthy industry of specialists who can repair the cars and supply parts. If it breaks (which it's unlikely to if it's well maintained), then you can mend it rather than throw it away. That's what I call a green car.

You *Can* Drive a Porsche

Ah, but a Porsche uses more fuel and pollutes more than a modern, efficient car, the critics will tell us. Possibly, although all Porsches in the UK since the early 1990s have been fitted with catalytic converters and have run on unleaded fuel since long before then. You have to remember that a 911 Turbo covering 7750 miles a year will produce less carbon dioxide than a Ford Fiesta driven 20,000 miles a year. If you're keen to reduce your carbon footprint (yes, I know it's a silly term) then drive your car less. In today's world of high-tech communication systems, it's mad to drive from your home to your office, simply to sit at a computer or talk into a phone, when you could be doing that just as well at home. There are plenty of people with modern, supposedly fuel-efficient cars but they do so many, often unnecessary, trips a year in them, that they negate any supposed environmental advantage. Generally, Porsches do not cover high annual mileages.

Even the environmentalists' dream car, the Toyota Prius, is less than green than you may think. An American company called CNW did research into the amount of energy cars used in their production, use and decommissioning and, guess what? The poor old Prius did worse than the 997-model 911! For the record, the Prius was 74th on the list of 96 cars, with the 997 Carrera 4 coming 61st and the Carrera 58th. And number

You *Can* Drive a Porsche

one on the list? This will surprise you – it was the Jeep Wrangler because of its traditional, low-tech manufacturing methods. Now, you may think that the Porsche 911 hasn't done that well in the league table, but you have to bear in mind that this does not take into account longevity; it assumes that a new 911 will have a lifespan of 151,000 miles, which in itself is better than the Prius's 100,000 miles. However, history shows that 911s keep going for much longer than that, with parts being replaced when they eventually wear out.

So there you have it; keeping an older car on the road can be better for the environment than dumping it and buying a new one every three years or so.

You *Can* Drive a Porsche

You *Can* Drive a Porsche

Getting permission

I help a lot of people find their dream Porsche and, very often, my clients are married men. During our initial conversations, I can guarantee that the wife will get mentioned. The usual comment goes along the lines of: "Well, my wife's given me the go ahead to buy a Porsche, but she thinks I'm mad."

This sort of comment always amuses me. First, because it's so predictable. Second, because it seems a bit sad that grown men feel they have to get permission. And, third, because their wives aren't more excited by the prospect of having a Porsche in the family.

I'm also surprised by the lengths some men go to hide the full extent of the purchase from their better halves. Some have blatantly lied about the cost of their new car, while others have weaved elaborate tales of trade-ins and finance deals to soften the blow.

Yet I'm sure these same men happily go out with their wives and buy new family saloon cars on expensive finance with crippling depreciation without batting an eyelid.

My favourite memory dates back some years, when I was writing an article on a heavily modified 911. The enthusiastic owner proudly gave me a breakdown of the money he'd spend on his pride and joy. He'd invested around £25,000 in the engine, suspension and bodywork. An incredible amount to spend on top of the purchase price, which was only about £20,000. He saw me making notes and his face fell. "You can't put that in the article," he groaned. "My wife doesn't know how much I've spent on the car. I explained that, really, I did need to tell the whole story, so he mulled it over for a while. With a smile he said: "Don't worry, I'll just make sure my wife doesn't see that issue of the magazine!" Now that is sad...

Generally, women are sensible with money and I can't see any reason why one wouldn't see the sense in spending money on a car that won't plummet in value. In fact, there are plenty of women who love driving Porsches so, if you're a man wondering what the missus will say, just get her to read this book. The only problem you may have, is that you'll find you'll never get your hands on the keys to the Porsche because she's too busy enjoying it. Two Porsche family, anyone?

Further reading

This little book is only intended as a short introduction to the Porsche marque and to get you thinking about a different and intelligent approach to car ownership.

Now I've whet your appetite, you'll no doubt want to know more, and there is a wealth of resources out there to help you. Here is just a small selection.

Philip Raby Porsche

Well, if I can't blow my own trumpet, who will? Has to be worth a visit!

www.philipraby.co.uk

Rennlist

A massive online Porsche community. Largely US-based but much of the information is relevant wherever you are www.rennlist.com

Impact bumpers

A friendly enthusiasts' forum dedicated to Porsche 911s built from 1974 to 1989 – the cars with the so-called impact bumpers.

www.impactbumpers.com

Porsche

Porsche's official website is, as you'd expect, very impressive and is worth a look, even if you can't afford a new Porsche

www.porsche.com

Porsche Club Great Britain

The largest Porsche Club in the UK.

www.porscheclubgb.com

The Independent Porsche Enthusiasts' Club

Or TIPEC to its friends

www.tipec.net

Autotrader

A great place to buy and sell Porsches. The online search facility is good.

www.autotrader.co.uk

Pistonheads

A popular motoring site with news and forums, but most useful for its free classified adverts.

www.pistonheads.com

You *Can* Drive a Porsche

About the author

I've been obsessed with cars since I was a young boy, and from an early age developed an affinity with Porsches, particularly 911s. I spent my teenage years rebuilding various cars from the ground up, learning how they work and what goes wrong with them.

I sell Porsches

I run my own Porsche sales business, based near Chichester in West Sussex, where I help people choose the right Porsche for them, and never give them a hard sell.

I write about Porsches

Over the years I have written for all the UK Porsche magazines, and was the founder of Total 911. I currently write a monthly column for GT Porsche magazine, and run my own blog

I'm a Porsche owner

Not surprisingly, I've owned several Porsches myself and currently drive a Cayenne.

You *Can* Drive a Porsche

And there's more...

I'm married with two wonderful children and we live on the wonderful south coast of England, where I love to spend my spare time sailing and cycling. It's a great life!

Do please get in touch if you'd like to chat about Porsches:

www.philipraby.co.uk

www.facebook.com/PhilipRabyPorsche

Twitter www.twitter.com/RabyPorsche

Printed in Great Britain
by Amazon